MYSTICAL JOURNEY

A Handbook for Modern Mystics

PETER MULRANEY

Copyright © 2019 by Peter Mulraney

All rights reserved.

No part of this book may be reproduced in any form or by any electronic or mechanical means, including information storage and retrieval systems, without written permission from the author, except for the use of brief quotations in a book review.

ISBN: 978-0-6482661-5-0

Cover image: Roy Son | Death to Stock

❦ Created with Vellum

To the ancient and modern mystics who inspire me.

CONTENTS

Introduction   vii

THE MYSTICAL JOURNEY

The mystical journey	3
Crossing the start line	5
Seek first the kingdom	8
Reality is not hidden	11
The way of not knowing	14
Life purpose	16
No-one special - just another pilgrim	18
10 ways of being for birthing a better world	20
Fellowship	24
Being the one	26

A MYSTIC'S TOOLKIT

Modern tools for modern mystics	31
Pausing	33
Meditation	35
Mandalas	38
Prayer	40
Allowing	43
Contemplation	45
Gratitude	47
Mindfulness	49
Uncovering beliefs	51
Embracing your creations	53
Forgiveness	55
I am affirmations	57
Immerse yourself in nature	59
Keeping a journal	61
Exercise	64
Sleep	65

The journey continues	67
A note from Peter	69
Also by Peter Mulraney	71

INTRODUCTION

I have been on the mystical journey for more than thirty years. As a self-confessed reluctant mystic, often held back by my fears and resistance to change, I recommit to the journey each morning.

I see myself as a Christian mystic. I grew up within a traditional Roman Catholic family and was an active member of my local parish well into my adult years. But things changed.

These days, when my friends call me a lapsed Catholic, I tell them I'm an evolved Catholic; one that has moved on from the theology of Rome; one that has chosen to seek answers to my questions beyond the confines of Church doctrine.

I believe there comes a time in life when you are called to question what you have been told is the truth, especially the truth about God and who you are. That's when the mystical journey starts. It can be a wild ride, and a lot of us decide not to take the chance and choose to stay within the safety of the herd. That's okay. God's patient and the call is always open.

People use terms like the 'dark night of the soul' to describe how it feels when you lose the certainties you thought you had but, like everything you encounter in life, that too will pass and, eventually, you will discover the truth that sets you free – if you persist.

I am a student of *A Course in Miracles* and the *Way of Mastery*, and I've been exposed to Buddhist and Sufi thought. When you read outside the sacred texts of your religious tradition, you discover there is only one truth expressed in many forms. There are many roads leading to the top of the mountain but the view from the top is the same, no matter how you get there.

I am what is called a modern or urban mystic. I don't live in a monastery. I'm married, have children, and live and work in my local community. My lifestyle is nothing like that of St Francis of Assisi, Mother Teresa, or any other saint.

This is a book for modern mystics like me, who walk a different pathway to the one followed by the holy men and women of history. The ancients, like St Francis of Assisi, got to hide away in monasteries and ashrams or a cave in the mountains. Today, we get to answer the call to the spiritual journey while walking the way of the householder in the streets, offices, shops, and factories of the world, right here where everybody else is.

In these pages, you'll find some insights into the mystical journey and a toolkit for navigating your way.

I encourage you to follow your heart and listen to your inner guidance. Let's begin.

THE MYSTICAL JOURNEY

THE MYSTICAL JOURNEY

The journey of a mystic is not about finding God. That's an impossible task.

That which is, otherwise known as God or a host of other names, reveals itself to anyone who takes the journey inspired by the question: Who am I?

That's the mystical journey.

The point of the mystical journey is not to find God but to become known by God, and the only way you can come to that is to know yourself.

The journey is a process of uncovering and remembering that looks like a process of learning and discovery, but it's a journey of unlearning and unmasking. It's a journey of coming out from behind your defensive shield. It's a journey of courage and vulnerability. It's a journey of integrating all aspects of yourself into wholeness.

The mystical journey cannot begin until you have lived a life you don't want. It's only when you realise you want something more or that you've been living someone else's dream or that you've settled for something less to survive that you're in a position to begin.

When that unsettling moment arrives, if you take the opportunity to spend some time exploring your doubts and questions, you may hear the call to embark on the journey. Or you may let your fears persuade you that it's better not to rock the boat or upset anybody.

But, God wants us all to begin. So, if you put it off, you may receive a more intense wake-up call, especially if you're reluctant to make changes in your life. For example: You get fired. Your spouse leaves you. You get sick. You lose all your money. Things stop working for you.

You have free will. So, when or whether you answer the call is your choice but, be warned, God is persistent.

The mystical journey is an inner journey. Your dragons live within, so that's where you need to go to meet them. It's a journey of death and resurrection where you put aside your old identity and take up a new one. It's a journey without end because who you are is forever expanding.

Your inner journey ultimately influences the expression of your outer journey. When you remember who you are, discover why you're here, and what gives you purpose, it's impossible to carry on as you have been living.

Going on the mystical journey always leads to transformation.

We all know this journey, which is why we're in love with stories, especially stories that embody the hero's journey.

All heroes are called to undertake the hero's journey and come to know themselves, and you are the hero in your life.

Maybe, this is not what you thought being a mystic was all about but, trust me, it is.

CROSSING THE START LINE

The mystical journey starts the day you wake up and wonder what is going on in your life.

That's the day you realise there has to be more to life than whatever you've been doing.

It's the day you start questioning whether what people are telling you is the truth. It's the day you stop being one of the herd.

That 'day' may dawn on you over a period of years or it may arrive as an unexpected life event you can't fail to notice.

For me, that day came when I was in my mid-thirties.

I walked away from a successful career in teaching and spent a year failing as an insurance agent before taking a year out of the workforce to be a stay-at-home father to our two small boys. Fortunately, my wife was able to rejoin the workforce and that allowed me the space to explore what was going on.

They were the outward signs. Inwardly, I was questioning my place in the world and my purpose in life. Those were the days of me describing my life as dull, colourless and boring. I didn't know what I wanted to do with my life or what I was supposed to be doing with it.

During that period, I discovered Transcendental Meditation and read *A Course in Miracles*. In fact, I spent that year working my way through the lessons of *A Course in Miracles* each morning after I'd taken the boys to school.

I don't remember how *A Course in Miracles* came to my attention. Maybe it was through Jerry Jampolsky's book *Love is Letting Go of Fear*, which I know I didn't purchase but ended up reading when I found it on the bookshelf.

The meditation practice introduced me to silence.

It took a while to get the hang of it. I'd sit for twenty minutes and really have no idea where I'd been. My awareness was going someplace my conscious mind couldn't or wouldn't go. It was very relaxing. It was an introduction to inner peace, a dimension without turmoil.

After a year studying *A Course in Miracles*, I could no longer hold onto some of the beliefs that had directed my life. That's when works by authors like Hans Kung, Matthew Fox, John Shelby Spong, Richard Rohr, John O'Donohue, Neil Douglas-Klotz, Jon Kabat-Zinn, Wayne Dyer, Tara Bach, Cynthia Bourgeault, Paul Ferrini, Eckhardt Tolle, Deepak Chopra, and Osho found their way into my library.

That was the first time I crossed the start line.

At the end of that year, I took a position in a bank, got interested in calligraphy, Celtic studies, and studied accounting. Even mystics have bills to pay, especially when they are parents of small children.

Life was happening on the surface but it was also happening in those unseen places when I meditated or read or discussed ideas with my wife. This was the period of being a reluctant mystic. I was on the path but I was dragging my feet and letting myself be distracted.

Then, a day came, several years later, when I needed something to read on a plane while I was flying interstate for work. That day I picked up a copy of *The Way of the Heart* magazine.

I'd been ambushed by Life.

In that magazine, I came across the *Way of Mastery* material which I've been working with ever since. It's not the only material I read but it's become my benchmark. It's from the same source as *A Course in Miracles* but it's written in a language I find easier to understand.

Years later, I realised I'd crossed another start line when I found myself writing the articles that became *My Life is My Responsibility: Insights for Conscious Living*.

Those words came from a dimension you can only access through meditation and listening. When I was writing those articles, it often felt like I was sitting at the computer watching words appear. That's an interesting feeling, knowing you have tapped into universal consciousness.

On reflection, I don't think you can stop the journey once you start, even if you think you can. I've been a reluctant mystic since the 1980s but, here I am, still on the path.

That still small voice is always talking to you even when you're doing your best to ignore it. In the end, you can't ignore it because it's the voice of Love calling you home, and Love is very persistent.

SEEK FIRST THE KINGDOM

In Matthew 6: 25 - 34, Jesus tells us to stop worrying about the things we think we need and to seek first the kingdom of God, knowing that the things we need will be given to us.

It takes us a while to get what Jesus means, partly because the message of mainstream Christianity is to be a good person, make the most of the circumstances you find yourself in, serve others, and pray you'll make it into the kingdom of God (heaven) when you die.

From my perspective, there is a mismatch between what Jesus advised us to do and what the Churches teach.

Jesus saw the kingdom of God as being present in the here and now, where we are. The Churches teach us the kingdom is in another space separate from where we are. A place you have to pass through the portal of death to reach.

We've had two thousand years of doing it according to the interpretations of Church leaders, and, for most of us, heaven is still some place we're hoping to get to when we die.

Taking the approach Jesus suggested is the way of the mystic.

The first step in seeking the kingdom of God is to stop worrying about what's going on in your life and to trust God. That's the message Matthew tried to pass on to us. In other words, stop trying to figure life out for yourself and let life unfold for you.

Stop keeping yourself busy. Stop worrying about money. Stop being anxious about your relationships. Take some time out, quieten your mind, and listen. That's how you create the space to allow the voice of God to direct your life.

Mystics are open to being guided, daily. But, becoming quiet enough to hear the voice within does not happen overnight. It requires an investment of time, which is why mystics talk about developing a meditation practice. A practice is something you do daily on an ongoing basis. This is the spiritual dimension of seeking first the kingdom.

The second step is to act as if you are living in the kingdom of God. This is the practical, pragmatic dimension of seeking first the kingdom, which works best if it's done in alignment with the spiritual work of listening.

When we think about living in the kingdom of God our minds tend to imagine utopia, a place of perfection, a paradise where all our needs are met.

Put aside all those images of beautiful places with just the right weather and consider the following aspects of life in the kingdom of God:

- All relationships are expressions of love.
- All acts are based in loving kindness.
- Everything operates for the highest benefit of all.
- You are always in the presence of God.

When you live in the kingdom, you allow God to flow through you and:

- you act out of love, no matter where you are or who you're with.
- you treat others with loving kindness because you are open-hearted.
- you consider the interests of others before you act.
- you are always aware of the presence of God.

You know what the world is like when we act out of self-interest and as if we belong to a privileged group entitled to exploit others and the planet. You only have to watch the news or read a newspaper if you need a reminder.

Mystics are called to live in the kingdom of God every day and to invite others to join them.

REALITY IS NOT HIDDEN

Reality is not hidden. It's in plain sight but it's not always visible to you.

Your mental filters block it from your awareness. In other words, you see what you choose to see. You see what you believe is happening.

We see with our minds, not with our eyes. We interpret everything we see within the framework of our beliefs and experience. We give meaning to the events and behaviours we encounter. We define our world from our point of view, according to what we know.

This means we never see reality - only our interpretation of reality.

You need to see with the heart to see reality. That means you have to clear the mind of beliefs and certainties, your mental filters, and allow reality to reveal itself to you.

In order to see the truth, you need to align your beliefs with reality and not with the world of your interpretations.

The question is: How can you do that?

Start by acknowledging your interpretations are clouded by your fears - which are only beliefs or stories that scare you.

Stop imposing or projecting your meaning onto people and events.

Be open to seeing things as they are and not as you want them to be.

Identify your beliefs, examine them closely, and test their validity. Question your assumptions. Investigate whether your beliefs and assumptions are evidence based or have simply been passed through to you by family, culture, and religion.

Consider this example of a belief passed to us through religion: 'I believe in God, the Father Almighty.'

Ever wondered how God got to be an almighty father figure after being worshipped as the earth mother for millennia? That's something to think about and do some research on if you'd like to know the answer.

Belief in an almighty God would have been an appealing idea to members of an oppressed tribe, as the Hebrews were in Egypt. Such a belief would allow people to console themselves with the thought that God would save them and, apparently, if you can believe what's in the Book of Exodus, he did.

But, if you look back on the history of the Jewish people over the last two thousand years, the Father Almighty has a fairly dismal track record when it comes to saving them.

Today, the Jewish nation of Israel relies on its military machine and that of the United States of America - and a lot less on Almighty God.

Does that personification of an all-powerful God still serve you in the world in which you live, or is it time to let that image go?

God is the I Am, the Source, the Void, All That Is - which means you are a part of God.

You are God being you to experience what you call your life.

Now, there's a truth you'll need to dissolve a few beliefs to see.

THE WAY OF NOT KNOWING

Not knowing scares us when we're waiting for something to happen and it's what stops us taking a leap of faith when we can't see a way forward.

We like certainty. We want to know. Knowing lets us feel safe. It lulls us into believing we're in control.

We invest a lot of energy in making sure we know what's going on, even in places far away. When we're on top of the news, it feels like we're in control of our lives. But is that true? I'm not so sure it's anywhere near the truth.

What do you really know?

The honest answer to that question is: not much, perhaps nothing at all.

Each time you breathe, you don't even know if you'll take another breath. You assume you will but there is no guarantee. Maybe that's why we try to ignore the process.

We know everybody dies but we have no idea when it will be our turn. Maybe that's why we're so afraid of dying. It's a known unknown. No wonder some people have trouble going to sleep each night.

When you experience a life event, is it better to interpret what's happening from your store of knowledge based on your past experience or to wait for the meaning of the event to unfold?

That part of your mind we call the ego always 'knows' what's going on. But that knowing is always an interpretation based on the past. It does not allow for any new developments or unknowns.

How many times are you surprised by the way things unfold when you allow them to happen without jumping to a conclusion? Ah, that's following the way of not knowing.

If you stop insisting you know, life can shower you with surprises, with miracles that are always available but invisible to the mind that knows.

If you want to experience those miracles, let go of all those certainties you entertain yourself with. You can't see what you insist is not there. You can't experience what you insist does not exist.

Trust creates the space for not knowing. Some of us think we have trust issues. People have let us down, betrayed our trust. We don't want to trust but there is no other way if we want to allow reality to unfold for us.

Whether we want to acknowledge it or not, we're all trusting the process of life. We're all trusting the universe will hold together and continue to support us. We're all trusting in a greater power even if we claim to be atheists.

It's time to put aside your certainties from the past and trust you'll be shown what you need to know in any life circumstance.

LIFE PURPOSE

There's a whole industry devoted to helping us discover our life purpose.

If you're anything like I was, when I first started thinking about my life purpose, you probably think your life purpose is something you have to do while you're here. Something important and fulfilling.

You know, something like saving the planet from global warming, eliminating poverty and injustice, ridding the world of single-use-plastic products, or finding a cure for cancer. All noble causes and great things to be involved in. I'm not saying not to do those things. They all need doing.

Most of us, though, are not in a position to engage with any of those tasks in a meaningful way. We can only contribute in small ways towards the achievement of those goals, for example, by not using plastic straws, composting our food waste, or funding organisations working to address those issues.

But what if your life purpose has nothing to do with what you do for a living?

What if your life purpose is to learn to love yourself?

We are not talking narcissism here. Rather, we're talking about loving yourself authentically, accepting yourself as you are, and treating yourself as the most important person in your life.

Sadly, although we want someone to love us like that, we fail to love ourselves in that same way. For some reason, we see ourselves as messed up, less than, and not worthy. Most of us find it a challenge to love ourselves.

That's why I think it's everyone's life purpose.

When you love yourself, your world changes. You stop putting yourself into harmful situations. You set boundaries. You take care of yourself. You come to realise you are your own best friend. And, you find it easier to love others because you are no longer needy for love, since you have tapped into the source of love within yourself.

I've noticed that people who love themselves love others and work to improve the world around them for the good of all.

I wonder how different our world would be if we set loving ourselves as our highest priority, instead of worrying about what we're doing with our lives.

If you're still wanting to find something fulfilling to do with yourself, choose something you enjoy doing which suits your talents and interests, and then love yourself while you do it.

NO-ONE SPECIAL - JUST ANOTHER PILGRIM

We all have roles in our families, communities, and workplaces. Each one of us takes on a range of roles in life. Some of us are leaders of nations or captains of industry. Others are teachers, farmers, priests or shop assistants. Some of us find ourselves as slaves or child-soldiers.

There are millions of roles to choose from and you get to choose several in the different spheres of your life while you're here.

The roles we take on often determine the circumstances of our lives. And, there is no denying that some lifestyles appear to be more attractive than others. There is nothing wrong with trying to improve your situation or the situation of others. That's one of the things love encourages us to do.

But, as far as embarking upon the mystical journey is concerned, no role is any better than any other. We are all called to the journey. We can all embrace the journey while we're doing whatever our role in the world entails.

However, when you answer the call and set out on the path, you soon realise that, no matter what your title is, you are no-one special - you're just another pilgrim on the way home.

If you experience feelings of superiority for being on a spiritual journey while your friends are still asleep, rest assured that's your ego speaking. It loves feeling special.

Smile, take a moment to breathe, and then remind yourself that all are equal in the eyes of God, who loves the sleepers just as much as the pilgrims.

10 WAYS OF BEING FOR BIRTHING A BETTER WORLD

 'Birds of a feather flock together.'

This is a bit of folk wisdom you're probably familiar with. Its origins come from observing the behaviour of birds. The wisdom part is a reflection on the tendency of people with similar beliefs and values to congregate together.

Take a look at the people you associate with. Don't be surprised if they hold similar beliefs and values to your own, and behave much the same way you do.

If you're not happy with your world, you can act on this folk wisdom to birth a new world for yourself by being the sort of person you want to be with.

BE PEACEFUL

The easiest way to live in a peaceful world is to be a peaceful person.

Stop fighting with people simply because you disagree with them. Listen instead of shouting them down. You might learn something and make a new friend instead of creating an enemy.

Being peaceful means choosing to stay unruffled when others question or oppose your point of view or disagree with your decisions.

Everyone is entitled to their opinion. You don't have to justify yours or demolish theirs. You can agree to disagree without starting world war three every time someone sees the world differently.

It takes courage and self-confidence to be peaceful but we all like being around a peaceful person. Why not be that peaceful person?

BE CONSIDERATE

One sure way to upset people is to do something that affects them without consulting them first. If you'd like people to show you some respect, the solution is to respect their feelings first.

Being considerate means thinking about the impact your actions may have on others and communicating with them before you act.

If you're in a personal or professional relationship, being considerate is how you show the significant others in your life they are important to you.

BE COMPASSIONATE

Being compassionate allows you to appreciate a situation from another person's point of view and consider their circumstances before acting. Compassion allows you to show genuine concern for others. Being compassionate is an expression of solidarity with others in your life. It's an expression of your humanity. It's a way of showing people your heart is open.

BE COLLABORATIVE

Being collaborative is how you signal you're a team player, whether that team is a work team, a family, or a partnership. It's about pitching in to help, lending a hand, or joining in a group effort to get something done.

We are social beings, and working together builds cohesion and a sense of belonging.

BE GENEROUS

Being generous means you're prepared to share your resources, knowledge, and skills for the benefit of others. In fact, you're prepared to give them away with no expectation of getting anything in return.

Being generous is acting from the realisation we are in this project of life together and get a better outcome when we share and lend each other a helping hand. When you're generous, you're saying you think of the welfare of others.

BE GRATEFUL

Being grateful is being able to say 'thank you' for whatever happens. Sometimes it's not easy, especially when things don't go the way you want, but every life circumstance holds something you can be grateful for. Better to look for that something than spend the rest of your days complaining.

Being grateful is simply remembering life is a gift and saying 'thank you' every day.

BE MINDFUL

Being mindful is paying attention to what's going on in your life as it's happening. It's about focusing on the task at hand and not time travelling down memory lane or into distant future scenarios. Being mindful enhances the enjoyment of living as it allows you to savour experiences instead of living through them while wishing you were somewhere else.

BE PRESENT

Being present is choosing to have your attention in the here and now. It's what allows you to hear what the person in front of you is saying, and not just with the words being spoken.

Being present is the ultimate gift you can give to another. It's how you say: I see you. I hear you.

It's also the ultimate gift you can give to yourself.

BE OPEN

Being open helps you to be peaceful as it allows for diversity. Being open-minded allows you to learn new things and enjoy new experiences. Being open-hearted allows you to be loving and compassionate. Being open allows things to flow through you and manifest in your world.

BE RESPONSIBLE

Being responsible is taking responsibility for your words, thoughts, and behaviours. It means no more blaming others for any aspect of your life. It means knowing you always have the power to choose how you will respond to any life event or any person's behaviour.

It means taking responsibility for choosing whether or not you are being any of the above.

FELLOWSHIP

The mystical path is solitary, in the sense that you are the only person who can do your spiritual or transformative work, but you don't need to do it alone.

Even those holy men and women we revere as saints lived in communities. We live in communities, too. We are surrounded by people who love us.

It's helpful if your partner in life or a close friend is also on the journey, since we all benefit from the fellowship of others going through what we are experiencing. Sometimes, all you have to do to find support is be willing to talk about what's going on in your life, and how you feel about it, with a friend who knows how to listen.

If you're on your own, though, seek out like-minded people through attending retreats and workshops. If there is no-one in your local area, sign up for an online group and join in the conversation.

When you do this work, your transformation may ruffle other people's feathers. Some will laugh, some will feel threatened, and others will disagree with you. That's why it's helpful to be part of a supportive community that understands your experience and appreciates your transformation.

BEING THE ONE

The point of the mystical journey is to open yourself to God and allow the love of God to flow through you to others. In the *Way of Mastery,* Jeshua tells us our purpose is to expand the good, the holy, and the beautiful. In other words, we are here to allow the expansion of love into and through the world of form.

Hopefully, by now, you understand that the mystical journey involves uncovering and removing all the blockages to the flow of God's love that you accumulated as you grew into a fully functioning human with a healthy ego personality.

As you identify and remove blockages, you gradually evolve into the one through whom God reaches out to others, which is why modern mystics are called to be with everyone else and not hidden away in a monastery or a cave in the hills.

Being the one means showing up and being present when you are with others. You don't have to know what to say or do but you do need to commit to giving your attention to that person or group of people. You will be guided as required, so be open to receiving that guidance.

Sometimes, you'll be surprised by what you say or do. There will be times when you won't realise what you have done, and you don't need to because it's not you doing it. You're simply being God's instrument.

When you're being the one, remember it's never about you. You're being the one for the other. They're the one that needs to hear the words, read the book you hear yourself suggest, or receive the hug you feel moved to give. Sometimes, you only have to listen and allow them to be heard and feel understood.

Being the one is holding space for others as they awaken and transform, which allows them to feel the presence of God.

A MYSTIC'S TOOLKIT

MODERN TOOLS FOR MODERN MYSTICS

Mystics have been around for thousands of years.

In times past, mystics were holy men and women that retreated to monasteries and ashrams, far away from the noise of the world, and ventured into the unknown seeking union with the divine. Most of those mystics were either members of religious orders or hermits, and we know a lot of them as saints.

For the ancients, being a mystic was solely an interior experience; something pursued within the solitude of a sacred space.

Modern mystics are people like you and me, and we find ourselves on a different spiritual journey to those who preceded us.

Although, like the mystics that came before us, we are called to hold space for the divine, we are also asked to walk openly among the throngs of humanity as conduits for divine energy. In other words, we are called to be open to the divine and to engage fully in being human where life is happening.

We are mystics walking the way of the householder in the streets, offices, shops, and factories of the world, right here where everybody else is.

Being a mystic in the modern world is not about seeking some ecstatic experience on a mountain top. It's about being fully present to your experience of life and attentive to those you are with. It's about letting your light shine for others to see, instead of hiding inside in a cloister, where it's safe.

Modern mystics are wayshowers, those called to awaken others and remind them they are more than they think they are.

We can't be wayshowers if we stay safely within a monastery or keep our insights to ourselves. We are called to walk with others where we can be seen and to live our insights in the here and now of everyday life. We are called to serve.

In the past, mystics relied on prayer, fasting, and isolation. Since modern mystics are called to embrace the experience of everyday life, they need access to tools appropriate for the times in which they live.

PAUSING

It's easy to ask questions like: Who am I? Why am I here? Are you there, God?

It's something altogether different to hear the answers to your questions. That requires silence and a willingness to listen.

You will not hear the voice of God until you make time to listen. That means pausing and taking a break from doing.

Modern people are addicted to doing. We keep ourselves busy to avoid examining what we're doing or questioning why we're living our lives the way we are. But, if you don't make the time to examine what's happening, you can't question your assumptions, you can't see your patterns, and you won't hear the guidance you ask for.

Mystics break that addiction by setting aside time for not doing.

There are many ways to pause and stop doing. Meditation and prayer, which I'll have more to say about later, are two ways of taking time out of your day to be still. A simple routine, like sitting quietly for ten to twenty minutes first thing in the morning or last thing at night, will help you establish a practice of pausing, of not doing.

Another approach is to schedule a time to check in with yourself on a regular basis, whether that's throughout your day, week, or month, to investigate how things are going in your life.

Another easy way to pause during the day is to bring conscious awareness to the act of breathing. This is a practice that brings your attention into the present moment, and you need to be present if you want to know what's going on. Taking a moment to breathe, whenever you're faced with a decision or potentially upsetting situation, gives you the space to respond based on what's going on instead of reacting automatically. It also creates a space for you to receive guidance before you decide or act.

Beyond daily pauses, taking extended breaks away from the normal activities of your life is a helpful habit. Retreat weekends away from home, for example, or a couple of weeks away from work doing things you enjoy with people you love, provide opportunities for getting in touch with yourself. And, getting in touch with yourself is a gateway to the divine.

Pausing is an aid to spiritual practice but it's also essential for maintaining physical and mental health. Being on a spiritual journey is not an excuse to ignore the health of your body and mind.

Pausing, which is discussed extensively in *The Pause Principle* by Kevin Cashman, is beneficial in all aspects of life, including work, business, and family. It's not something just for mystics - but it is a practice of all mystics.

MEDITATION

One of the first steps on the road of the spiritual journey is slowing down and learning to sit and do nothing.

This is a major challenge for a lot of us. We've grown up in a society where we are encouraged to keep ourselves busy. In fact, a lot of us are actually addicted to activity, or our devices, and don't ever give ourselves any down time.

Even when you're doing nothing in particular there is a voice in your head, that sounds a lot like your father's, mother's, or some teacher's from your childhood, telling you that you should be doing something.

That voice has been driving your decision making since you first heard it, and it will continue to do so until you develop sufficient self-awareness to stop listening to it.

Meditation is a way of developing the self-awareness which will set you free from your conditioning.

When I first started looking into meditation, I was under the misperception that it was a religious activity. It can be, but it doesn't have to be.

The type of meditation I practice these days is called Mindfulness Meditation. It may have its roots in Buddhism, but you don't have to take on any beliefs to practise it. *Waking Up: Searching for Spirituality Without Religion* by Sam Harris, scientist, philosopher and skeptic, is an interesting read if you're worried about the religious aspect of meditation.

If you're particularly religious, follow a meditation practice aligned with your religion - they all have one - because all practices lead to the same place in the end.

The simplest form of meditation I know is something you can try right now. Put the book down, sit comfortably in a chair, close your eyes, and just notice your breathing. Focus your attention on your breath and let any thoughts that come into your awareness float by, like clouds in the sky of your mind. If you realise you have chased a thought down a rabbit hole, simply bring your awareness back to your breathing. When you've had enough, slowly open your eyes and bring your attention back into the room.

When you first start meditating, you may find it difficult to sit still for even ten minutes at a time. Some people go to sleep well before ten minutes are up. Don't panic, and don't give up if that happens to you. It's fairly normal. If you snore, you'll wake yourself up, eventually - I did.

Start with ten minutes, and gradually increase the amount of time you meditate up to twenty or thirty minutes. Many teachers recommend meditating for twenty minutes two times a day but once is enough when you're starting.

Set yourself a goal of meditating every day for 30 days to allow it to become a regular practice, a part of your daily routine.

You can set the timer on your smartphone to remind you when the time is up. A gentle chime works best.

There is a wealth of material on meditation available online and in bookstores which you can tap into, and there are many meditation centres around the world where you can learn to meditate.

MANDALAS

A mandala is a diagram, made of repeated symbols or patterns. Constructing mandalas has a long history as a meditation aid.

In our busy lives, where many of us struggle to find the time to meditate or enjoy some down time, coloring mandalas is one way of slowing down and taking a moment for yourself.

You can spend as little as a few minutes a day coloring or as long as it takes to complete a mandala in one sitting. The mind thinks you're doing something, so it's okay with you spending time doing it.

The secret to mandalas is in the process. It's the actual coloring itself and not the end result that is the important part.

Coloring a mandala is a gateway process for entering a meditative state. It's a relatively easy way to start a meditation practice, especially if you find sitting still in silence a challenge.

All you need is a mandala diagram, a handful of colored pencils, a pencil sharpener and an open mind. You can draw your own or color in a pre-drawn mandala.

There are plenty of books available with pre-drawn mandalas for you to color in, including one I designed: *Sharing the Journey Coloring Book: Mandalas*.

Like all forms of meditation, coloring mandalas works best if you do it regularly. Give it a go, especially if you're having trouble establishing a regular meditation practice, and give yourself permission to color outside the lines. It's not about creating an art masterpiece; it's about freeing the mind from its everyday concerns while you work on the mandala.

PRAYER

Most of us know about prayers of intercession - prayers asking God for something. We have prayer books full of such prayers, yet the secret all mystics know is the prayer of silence.

There is nothing wrong with asking but the point of prayer is not to give God your shopping list of desires. God knows what you need. That was the point Jesus was making when he advised us to seek first the kingdom.

Prayer starts with attuning to the divine. Attuning is an activity that takes us out of our normal world and into the presence of the divine.

Sacred chanting is a method of attuning with the divine. If you've ever heard Buddhists monks chanting 'Om' or Christian monks using Gregorian chant you know what I mean. If you don't, try an internet search using 'sacred chants' to explore the world of chanting.

Indigenous people all over the world use sacred chanting, often accompanied by drumming. This is simply a way of opening up the communication channels to the divine on an appropriate frequency. If you are a churchgoer, this is why the service often starts with singing.

Listening to sacred music also allows you to attune with the divine.

If sound is not your thing, you can use conscious or yogic breathing to move into a space beyond your normal existence and attune with the divine. To do this, sit quietly or lie down with your eyes closed and focus on your breathing. Notice the rhythm of your normal breathing. Then, expand the in breath for a count of 5 and immediately rollover into the out breath for a count of 5 and repeat for several minutes before returning to normal breathing.

Prayer is communicating with the divine - and it's not a one-way street. You also need to listen. Once you've set your intention, asked for guidance, and opened a channel through attunement, it's time for silence on your part.

By taking the time to attune and be silent you are signalling your willingness to listen. God's answer may not come straight away, it may come when you think you are no longer praying, but it will come.

God does not talk in a loud voice. That's your ego. God talks in silence. Sometimes that silence delivers an insight. Sometimes it allows you to hear the voice of God speaking to you through the person you're with or the book you're reading. Often, God's response is simply the way your life unfolds, so pay attention.

There will be times when that answer only becomes obvious on reflection. That's part of your prayer life too.

Prayer is not something reserved for special occasions or Sundays. You can pray in groups and you can pray alone in your room whenever you choose. A meditation practice is a gateway to prayer you can walk through every day. God is always there.

That's something else mystics know: you are always in the presence of God, even when you think you're not.

ALLOWING

An essential practice for mystics is allowing life to unfold.

Life unfolds and reveals itself continually. Despite our protestations, we have no control over the process or the flow of events or people that pass through our realm of experience.

The opposite of allowing is resistance, attempting to stop the flow. Resistance, the root cause of suffering, is energy draining and all teachers of the journey advise us to give it up.

Even in times past, when mystics withdrew from the world, they could not escape from the unfolding of life. No-one can stop the process. Allowing is one of their tools that is still relevant today.

Modern mystics, immersed in the world, may be exposed to more events, more unexpected outcomes, and more temptations to resist, but the process of allowing is the same.

Allowing is a form of surrender to the flow of God's plan for your life.

When something challenging comes along, whether it be a setback or someone leaving, instead of resisting or voicing your disappointment, wonder why you're having that experience. Let the event unfold without investing energy in resistance.

You may have to sit with it, pray about it, or sleep on it, but its significance will become apparent if you allow it to come to you.

It helps if you appreciate that life happens for you and not to you. In other words, life is allowing you to unfold and evolve through the events and relationships it brings to you.

Your task is to notice what's happening and be grateful for the flow of life. As a mystic, you are called to respond from understanding and not react from ignorance.

When you allow all things, you have more energy available for living.

Allowing is going with the flow and enjoying the ride as you discover where life is taking you.

In my experience, it's much easier to go willingly than to be dragged along resisting with every breath.

CONTEMPLATION

One of the pitfalls of modern life is quick decision making - accepting things or people at face value instead of delving into them and becoming properly informed before deciding. We tell ourselves we don't have the time to process a full assessment. Life is too busy.

Accepting things at face value is a recipe for frustration and disappointment because things and people are often not what they seem. Fortunately, there is an alternative: contemplation.

Contemplation is giving deep reflective thought to things over time. It's the opposite of quick decision making.

Contemplation is spending time discerning the meaning of life events. It's taking your time coming to a decision. It's working out whether some new idea resonates with you or whether some old belief no longer serves you.

There are times when you need to make quick decisions, for example, when you're driving, playing sport, or your child steps into harm's way. Making quick decisions in appropriate circumstances is an essential life skill.

But, there are times when a considered decision is more appropriate, for example, when you start a career, decide to get married, change jobs, vote, or update your beliefs. Not everything in life has to be rushed.

Contemplation is a constructive use of that quiet time we discussed in the chapter on pausing, especially when you're faced with major change in your life.

GRATITUDE

Every life experience has something for you, even those that initially don't look so good when they arrive. Being grateful doesn't mean you have to enjoy a disaster when it happens but it does mean being open to the lesson embedded within that disaster - even if it's only a reminder that you don't want that experience anymore.

In the *Way of Mastery*, Jeshua reminds us that if we don't like what's going on in our lives, it's time to choose again. It's time to think about life differently so we can attract a different set of circumstances. Gratitude allows us to say thanks for the reminder.

Gratitude is both an attitude and a daily practice. Expressing appreciation for the people and things in your life is a way of acknowledging that your life is unfolding for you and is not simply a series of events happening to you.

It's difficult to be grateful and think of yourself as a victim at the same time. A victim's response is to blame and complain. Being grateful helps you move away from seeing yourself as a victim. It's also a way of expressing your trust in the promise that God will look after you and provide all those things you need in life.

An easy way to develop gratitude is to list three things you are grateful for in your journal each day before you go to bed. You don't have to limit yourself to three things. Remember your gratitude for the people in your life, and not just the ones you live with. Think of all the people that do things behind the scenes that allow your life to happen. Be grateful for them and what they do for you.

And, finally, remember to be grateful for the gift of life.

MINDFULNESS

Another word for mindfulness is attentiveness. Being mindful is simply paying attention to what's going on in the present moment or of being present to the now - where your life is happening.

Watch a child at play, especially one playing on its own. Children give their whole awareness to what they are doing.

By the time we become adults, most of us have lost our sense of mindfulness. We are easily distracted by our concerns and, often, there is a disconnect between the location of our bodies and the focus of our minds.

Fortunately, mindfulness is a skill you can recapture by slowing down and paying attention to who or what is in front of you. It helps if you do one thing at a time and give up multitasking.

The great benefit of mindfulness is becoming aware of what you are thinking, saying, or doing in the moment you are thinking, saying, or doing it. That's how you become aware of what's really going on. It's how you become aware of the assumptions you make, especially when you wonder why you're doing what you're doing or saying what you're saying.

The focus of mindfulness is the present moment, the most important moment there is, since it's where your life is happening. If you really want to engage in life, it stands to reason that your mind and body need to be in the same place at the same time.

Mindfulness is a practice, it's a level of awareness you make a commitment to maintaining. You'll slip and time travel into the past or the future. We all do, despite the best of intentions. But, when you notice you've let your mind wander, take a breath and bring your focus back to the present moment.

Do it often enough and you'll always be present. You'll also be more productive, more empathetic, and more loving.

It's surprising how different the world is when you pay attention.

A book on mindfulness worth looking into is *Wherever You Go There You Are* by Jon Kabat-Zinn.

UNCOVERING BELIEFS

No-one operates in this world without a set of beliefs. If you want an insight into what you believe, take a look at the circumstances of your life. They reflect your current beliefs.

A few starting questions:

- Who are you with? What sort of people do you surround yourself with? How do you let people treat you?
- Where do you live? What have you surrounded yourself with? What does that tell you about how you treat yourself?
- What thoughts guide your decisions? Do you believe in scarcity and limitation or abundance and possibilities? Do you make assumptions about other people?
- What do you say to yourself every day? Listen to your 'I am statements' and write them down. Capturing them on paper will allow you to see what you believe about yourself and your place in the universe.
- Are you living in a safe or scary world? Do you trust people? Or is the world out to get you? Is your life one of peace or anxiety?

If you don't examine your life, you will never know if what you believe is evidence based or simply someone's unquestioned opinion - and all of us have been indoctrinated by our cultures, religions, institutions, and the media.

It's tempting to stay with the familiar awareness of the group consciousness installed by your cultural and religious indoctrination. In fact, you will experience varying levels of resistance from friends, family, and strangers when you choose not to. You need to be ready for that. Not everyone will support your questioning of the status quo. Some will find it confronting but that is not your problem. You are on your journey. They are on theirs.

As mystics, we are called to awaken to a level above the default setting of awareness that is mass consciousness. To do that requires uncovering your beliefs, and becoming aware of the default assumptions and prejudices that come into play whenever you make a decision or pass judgement on the actions of others.

You will make no progress on your journey of self-discovery until you uncover your beliefs. This is not something you will do in an afternoon or over a weekend. Uncovering beliefs is an ongoing activity. It requires mindful attention to your thoughts, words, and actions. It requires looking into parts of the mind you'd rather not venture into, those parts where your dragons reside. This is an activity for journal work.

Once you uncover the beliefs you have been operating under, start stepping outside your belief bubble and explore other possibilities. Read widely, take courses, talk to people, and be curious.

A useful resource for working with beliefs is *Liminal Thinking* by Dave Gray.

EMBRACING YOUR CREATIONS

Embracing your creations as a way of returning to original wholeness is one of the concepts discussed by Jeshua in the *Way of Mastery*.

This is also known as shadow work. This is the part of the spiritual journey we all like to put off because it involves confronting and owning all those aspects of ourselves that we don't really want to know or admit exist - those dragons we all have locked in the basement of our subconscious minds.

Embracing your creations is where you work with your fears and all your misdeeds and come to own them. This is where you search out all your fragmented parts and gather them into yourself to return to original wholeness. This is where you realise there is no good or bad. There are just experiences you have labelled. Fortunately, you can erase those labels and choose to look at those aspects of yourself differently.

Shadow work is covered in *The Way of Transformation* in the *Way of Mastery* course, but there are other resources you can turn to for guidance, for example, *Integrate the Shadow: Master Your Path* by Dr Matthew B James, *Bringing Your Shadow Out of the Dark* by

Robert Augustus Masters, or *The Secret of the Shadow: The Power of Owning Your Story* by Debbie Ford.

There is no way around this part of the journey. This is where heroes make friends with their dragons because they recognise them as parts of themselves.

Shadow work is another activity that lends itself to working with a journal.

FORGIVENESS

The idea of forgiveness is a hurdle until you realise the only person you have to forgive is yourself.

All of your grievances are imagined, since they are based on your misinterpretation of events and other people's intentions. Forgiving yourself for your misinterpretations allows you to release people from your distorted view of them and see them as they are.

We use our interpretations of people's intentions to imagine all sorts of slights and hurts. Your partner, for example, says something that you hear as hurtful. You see attack. You feel violated or taken for granted.

All your partner did was utter a string of words. That's a neutral event - until you invest it with an interpretation.

If instead of asking for clarification, you assume you know what they intended, you end up making a judgment based on a misinterpretation.

When our relationships become strained under the weight of our misinterpretations, we feel a need to forgive in order to restore them. The temptation is to be magnanimous, to offer the olive branch and forgive the other for their one or many transgressions.

This is not how forgiveness works.

When you attempt to forgive that way, you end up feeling resentful for swallowing your pride again. You've let them off when what you wanted was an apology. You know you only did it to restore the peace. You still feel that you were right and that, once again, you've been the greater person.

To forgive, acknowledge your misinterpretations and forgive yourself for projecting them onto the other. Doing that allows you to release the other from your judgments and become willing to see them as they are. Prepare yourself for some pleasant surprises as you forgive yourself.

From the perspective of one who accepts responsibility, feeling hurt or offended is a response you choose.

Instead of holding on to your hurt and projecting it on to others, wonder why you chose to respond that way in the first place.

Finding the underlying reason for your misinterpretation is a first step towards responding differently next time. And, there will be a next time. How else will you know whether you've learnt that particular lesson?

I AM AFFIRMATIONS

I am affirmations are statements of belief. We use them all the time, often unthinkingly, to reinforce our beliefs about who we are.

Spend some time listening to the I am statements you make. Write them down so you can see what you are saying about yourself. If you're like most people, you'll be shocked by the number of negative I am statements you repeat to yourself every day.

Now, consider some positive I am statements you could use instead. For example:

- I am amazing
- I am beautiful
- I am creative
- I am decisive
- I am energetic
- I am free
- I am grateful
- I am happy
- I am imaginative
- I am joyful

- I am kind
- I am lovable

Don't just read them. Say them out loud and notice how you feel about saying positive statements about yourself. Does that surprise you?

When you work with I am affirmations, it's not uncommon for your negative beliefs to rise to the surface of your awareness in opposition to the positive statements you are using to describe yourself. You may even hear your ego voice challenging those affirmations. Don't let that discourage you. It means the affirmations are working.

I am affirmations are a useful tool for flushing out your negative beliefs about yourself for examination - useful fuel for your shadow work.

The secret is to stop saying those negative things about yourself once you're aware of them. And, let them go without berating yourself when you fall back into your old habits. Habits are hard to break and it's normal to slip back into your old ways whenever you start something new. Be kind to yourself and simply recommit.

Consciously using positive I am statements allows you to think about yourself differently - if you persist. Remember, you're worth it.

To succeed, you need to make it a habit that replaces your old way of talking about yourself negatively, and that requires commitment and self-discipline. Give it a 30 day trial.

My book *I Am Affirmations: The Power of Words* contains a collection of 81 positive affirmations if you need more to work with.

IMMERSE YOURSELF IN NATURE

Some days you simply need to spend time in nature. Especially on those days when it feels like your life is too much to deal with.

On a day like that, get out of the house and stroll through the park. Walk on the beach or down by the river. Sit in the garden. Breathe and open all your senses to the natural world. Relax and soak it all in.

The modern world is a place of continual movement and noise, especially if you live in a city. When I lived in New York, it was almost impossible to find a quiet spot. There was no escape from the sirens and the ever-present helicopters, even in the middle of Central Park.

To meditate in such a place, you have to stop regarding sounds as noise. All those things you call noise need to become sounds in the environment you can choose to either pay attention to or allow to fade away into insignificance. Yes, it takes practice but it can be done. If you have ever worked in an open-plan office, you'll know what I mean or have a technique to experiment with.

Walking through a forest far from the sounds of the city or along a beach being inundated by breaking waves transports you into a reality far removed from your daily grind. It gives you an opportunity to refresh your mind, release your cares, and soak in the energy always available to you.

In Japan, they call immersing yourself in nature forest bathing and you can join a group to walk through a forest. It's a phenomenon catching on in the West, where you can go trekking or hiking in your local woods with a guide.

But, you don't have to go that far. You can gift yourself a nature bath simply by sitting in a green space and drinking in the energy of nature.

If there is nothing natural in your immediate environment, befriend a pot plant or stop to watch the sunset from your window.

There is so much beauty in the natural world you can tap into to regenerate yourself.

Stop ignoring it.

KEEPING A JOURNAL

Keeping a journal is one way of creating a reliable written record for reflection.

In a journal, you can create a record of the events that make up your daily life, and your reflections on those events or on the greater questions of life you ask when seeking meaning.

If you meditate, you can use a journal to record your insights.

You can also use a journal to problem solve or record your dreams.

If you like doodling, a journal is as good a place as any to store your doodles.

A journal is a place where you can safely design the life you want to lead, while you're developing the courage to change your behaviour and beliefs. Reflecting on what you record in your journal helps you unearth patterns in your behaviour and beliefs, which is useful when you're doing shadow work.

Like a caterpillar that goes into its chrysalis to work on its transformation into a butterfly, you can go into your journal to complete the work required to fuel your own transformation.

And, remember, you're the only person who needs to be able to read it.

Often, it's the act of writing that does the work, and maybe you'll never reread what you write. There are plenty of pages in my journals I have trouble reading, so heaven help anyone who stumbles across them when I'm gone.

You can start journaling by asking yourself some questions and then writing down whatever answers come up. The secret is not to think about it too much or edit what you write. Just write - sometimes the answers really surprise you.

A few starter questions:

- What do I believe in?
- What could I live without?
- What can't I live without?
- What hurts am I holding on to?
- What do I want to do with my life?
- What are my special talents and qualities?
- How do I feel about (a specific event or person)?
- Why did (a specific event or person) show up in my life?

Journal work can be challenging, so it's often helpful to work with some guidelines from others who have gone before us. You might find the following books useful starting places: *Your Ultimate Life Plan* by Jennifer Howard, *Change Your Thoughts, Change Your Life* by Wayne Dyer, *Real Happiness* by Paul Ferrini, and *Love is Letting Go of Fear* by Jerry Jampolsky.

Another approach to journal work is to write out the story of your life. You don't have to share it with anyone but yourself - unless you want to publish a memoir. We're all carrying around the story of everything that has ever happened to us - the good, the bad, and the ugly. Using a journal is one way of getting in touch with that story.

One resource for really getting in touch with your story is *Writing from the Heart* by Nancy Aronie.

For some reason, journaling works best if you use a pen and paper, so get yourself a decent exercise book, visual diary, or purpose designed journal.

As a long-time journal keeper, I recommend the practice.

EXERCISE

With all this discussion of pausing and meditating, it's easy to perceive the mystical journey requires spending a lot of quiet time sitting on a cushion. It can be like that but it doesn't have to be that way. And, even when it is, your body is still going to need some exercise to make up for all that sitting.

There is no requirement for mystics to be sedentary, and it's a good idea to engage in physical exercise for the general well-being of your body in any case. You don't have to train like an Olympic athlete but you can if you want to. The secret to exercise is moving your body on a regular basis, whether that's going for a walk, cycling, playing sport, or going to the gym.

There are some forms of physical exercise that serve both as vehicles for promoting your general well-being and enhancing your meditation.

A few worth exploring are:

- Walking meditation
- Yoga
- Tai Chi, and
- Qigong

SLEEP

As modern mystics we are engaged with the world. We have families and jobs, and the responsibilities that go along with them.

The pace of modern living is hectic. And, often, it seems there simply aren't enough hours in the day to get everything done. When we feel time poor, we're tempted to burn the candle at both ends and spend less hours sleeping. This leads to sleep deprivation.

If you're interested, there's plenty of information available online about the effects of sleep deprivation. Let me just say here that there is no information saying it's good for you.

The work of personal transformation, especially when it involves releasing past hurts, is tiring. It's a good idea to allow ample time for rest and relaxation when you're processing what comes up during shadow work.

There is no point in working on yourself if it turns you into a grump through lack of sleep. There is no rush, the journey you are on is continuous. There is no endpoint where you get to say you have arrived.

So, look after yourself along the way and make sure you get plenty of sleep. You'll be much more fun to be around when you do.

THE JOURNEY CONTINUES

I hope you find the insights and tools presented in *Mystical Journey* as useful on your journey as I find them on mine.

As mentioned in the text, there is no end to the mystical journey. I've been on my journey for more than thirty years and I'm still learning things about myself and the ways of the universe.

Use this handbook to guide you on your way but don't restrict yourself to its contents. Yes, it's a distillation of insights from thirty years of contemplation but they are my insights. I have shared them with you as that's what I've felt called to do. But, I'm not infallible. I'm a pilgrim on the path, and there are many others like me with insights to share.

No one of us ever has all the answers, and I advise you to be on your guard if you encounter someone who claims they do. I'm fully aware I only have a partial appreciation of the big picture and I'm always open to new information, to new ways of doing things.

The journey is often a challenge. Things don't always go to plan. Sometimes it feels like all your meditation, prayer, and loving kindness makes no difference. Horrible things still happen despite your efforts to birth a better world. On those days, I encourage you to recommit to the journey - because that's making a recommitment to yourself.

When you find yourself feeling down or defeated by life, take courage. Trust the process. All things pass, and underneath all of the darkness you will always find love if you allow it to enter your world.

Peace be with you.

Peter Mulraney.

A NOTE FROM PETER

Mystical Journey: A Handbook for Modern Mystics is my fourth book of insights. I hope you enjoy working with the insights and receive a few of your own.

I see sharing these insights, which have come to me over years of meditation and study, as part of my life's work. You can help create a greater awareness of them by writing a review and telling your friends about the book.

You can find details about my other books and read my blog on www.petermulraney.com, where you can subscribe to my monthly newsletter 'Insights from a crime writing mystic' and download a free copy of *A Question of Perspective*.

Get in touch.
www.petermulraney.com
peter@petermulraney.com

ALSO BY PETER MULRANEY

Writings of the Mystic

Sharing the Journey: Reflections of a Reluctant Mystic

A Question of Perspective (Paperback)

My Life is My Responsibility: Insights for Conscious Living

I Am Affirmations: The Power of Words

Beyond the Words: Reflections on I Am Affirmations

Sharing the Journey Coloring Books

Mandalas

Mandalas by 3

Sharing the Journey Coloring Journals

Sharing the Journey Coloring Journal

Sharing the Journey Coloring Journal ~Discovery

Sharing the Journey Coloring Journal ~ Reflection

Crime fiction and self-help

Peter Mulraney also writes crime fiction and self-help. You can sample all of his books in his free Official Reading Guide.